MEN-OF-WAR

W.W. NORTON & COMPANY

NEW YORK / LONDON

MEN-OF-WAR

Patrick O'Brian

The text of this book is composed in Sabon
with the display set in Sabon (distorted)
Composition by ComCom
Manufacturing by Impresora Donneco International, S.A. de C.V.
Book design by Jam Design

Library of Congress Cataloging-in-Publication Data

O'Brian, Patrick, 1914–
Men-of-war / Patrick O'Brian.—1st American ed.
p. cm.
Includes index.
1. Ships of the line—History—18th century. 2. Seafaring life—
History—18th century. I. Title.
V795.027 1974
359.3′22′094109033—dc20   95-2297

ISBN 0-393-03858-0

W. W. Norton & Company, Inc., 500 Fifth Avenue, New York, N.Y. 10110
W. W. Norton & Company Ltd., 10 Coptic Street, London WC1A 1PU

1 2 3 4 5 6 7 8 9 0

Contents

Acknowledgments

The publishers are grateful to the National Maritime Museum, London for the use of the photographs in this book. Pictures not provided by the Museum are from the following sources: page 20, Special Projects Unit, *The Sunday Times*; page 23, Crown Copyright, The Science Museum, London; page 35, William Collins Sons & Co. Ltd.; page 90, The National Gallery, London.

Introduction

Since Britain is an island, it has always needed a navy to keep enemies from coming over the sea to invade it. If there had been an efficient navy in Roman times neither Caesar nor Claudius could have crossed the Channel; if there had been one in 1066, William would never have been called the Conqueror; and if there had *not* been one in the Armada year the British might be speaking Spanish now. Without the Royal Navy to stop him, Napoleon would certainly have invaded England in 1805 (he had 2,293 vessels in the Channel ports ready to carry 161,215 men and 9,059 horses across), just as Hitler would have done in 1940.

Then again, since England has been a trading nation time out of mind, it has always needed a navy to protect its merchant ships and to attack the enemy's sea-borne trade. And ever since England became an industrial country as well, unable to produce enough food for its greatly increased population, a navy has been essential to prevent its being starved into surrender.

A navy has always been necessary; but it was not for many centuries after King Alfred's time that the Royal Navy as we know it, a permanent service quite separate from the mercantile marine, came into being. The kings generally had some ships of their own, but in war most of the country's naval force was made up of merchantmen, some hired and some provided by such towns as the Cinque Ports; and once the war was over they went home: they were not real men-of-war, in the sense of being ships specially built and armed for fighting alone. "Man" is an odd word for a ship, since sailors call all vessels "she", but "man-of-war" came into the language about 1450, and it has stayed, together with East-Indiaman for a ship going to India or Guineaman for one sailing to West Africa, and many more. Henry VIII had about fifty men-of-war, and it was he who set up the Admiralty and Navy Board to look after them. Queen Elizabeth I had fewer—of the 197 English ships that sailed to fight the Spanish Armada only 34 belonged to her. Charles I had 42, but in the wars of the Commonwealth the number grew, so that when King Charles II came into his own again he had 154 vessels of all kinds. It was at this time that the Navy began to take on its modern shape: formerly the King had had to keep his ships out of his own pocket, but now the nation paid for them; and now the officers, instead of being sent away when there was no need for them, were kept on half-pay—they could make a career of the Navy rather than join from time to time. This did not apply to the men, however: they came aboard, or were brought aboard by the press-gang, every time there was a war; and when it was over they went back to their former ways of making a living. By the end of Charles II's reign the Royal Navy had 173 vessels, and because of the labours of Samuel Pepys, the Secretary of the Admiralty, and of the Duke of York, who was Lord High Admiral, it was a fairly efficient body.

All through the eighteenth century the Royal Navy grew: in

1714 there were 247 ships amounting to 167,219 tons; in 1760 412 of 321,104 tons; and in 1793, although the number had dropped by one, the tonnage amounted to 402,555. This was at the beginning of the great war with France, in which the Royal Navy reached the height of its glory, and the numbers increased rapidly; by the time Napoleon had been dealt with, Britain had no less than 776 vessels, counting all she had taken from the French, Spaniards, Danes and Dutch; and altogether they came to 724,810 tons. At this time, at its greatest expansion, the Royal Navy needed 113,000 seamen and 31,400 Royal Marines, and a hard task it was to find them, as we shall see when we come to the press-gang.

The Ships

T he vessels that made up the early Navy were of all shapes and sizes, from Henry VIII's *Henry Grace à Dieu* of 1,000 tons down to row-barges, passing by cogs, carracks, and ballingers, shallops and pinnaces; but by the seventeenth century the pattern that lasted up until the coming of steam was clear, and by the eighteenth it was firmly established. The ships of the Royal Navy were divided into six rates as early as Charles I, and this is how they stood in 1793:

first rate	100–112 guns, 841 men (including officers, seamen, boys and servants)
second rate	90–98 guns, 743 men
third rate	64, 74 and 80 guns, 494, about 620, and 724 men
fourth rate	50 guns, 345 men (this rate also included 60-gun ships, but there was none in 1793)
fifth rate	32, 36, 38 and 44 guns, 217–297 men
sixth rate	20, 24 and 28 guns, 138, 158 and 198 men.

All these ships, from 20 to 112 guns, were commanded by post-captains.

The *Hermione*, a 12-pounder 32-gun frigate—that is to say, she carried 32 guns that fired 12-pound balls as her main armament. You can see her starboard broadside of great guns run out, but the smaller weapons, such as carronades, on her quarterdeck and forecastle, are hidden by the fighting. The crew of the *Hermione*, driven to despair by a brutal captain, had mutinied and carried the ship into a port on the Spanish Main, where the Spaniards took her into their navy. Some time later Captain Hamilton of the *Surprise*, a 28-gun frigate, found her moored in Puerto Cabello and protected by strong batteries on shore. He could not take his ship in, so he hoisted out his boats that night and boarded her. While the fighting was going on on deck, some of the *Surprise*'s men ran aloft and loosed the foretopsail (the picture shows it beginning to fill) and others cut the cables: the *Hermione* moved out to sea, beyond the reach of the batteries, and a little after midnight she belonged to the Royal Navy again.

Vessels that carried less than 20 guns—that is to say, all the sloops, brigs, bomb-ketches, fire-ships, cutters and so on—were not rated, and their captains were masters and commanders in the case of sloops, and lieutenants in the rest. ("Captains" in the sense of commanding officers, not of permanent rank: if a midshipman was sent away in charge of a prize, he was her captain so long as he was in command.)

The ships that carried 60 guns and more were called ships of the line, because it was they alone that could stand in the line of battle when two fleets came into action. The first and second rates were three-deckers (that is to say they had three whole decks of guns, apart from those on the quarterdeck and forecastle); the third and fourth rates and the 44s were two-deckers; and the rest one-deckers—they were frigates from 38 guns down to 26, and post-ships when they carried 24 or 20. The word frigate was used in the seventeenth century without any very precise meaning, but by this time it had long been understood to mean a ship that carried her main armament on one deck and that was built for speed: the frigates were the eyes of the fleet, and they were also excellent cruisers, capital for independent action.

In 1793, counting those that were being built or repaired, those that were laid up and those that were stationary harbour ships, the Royal Navy had 153 ships of the line, 43 50- and 44-gun two-deckers, 99 frigates, and 102 unrated vessels.

I say vessels rather than ships because, although a vessel means anything that floats or is meant to float, for a sailor a ship is something quite distinct: it is a vessel, of course, but it is a square-rigged vessel with three masts (fore, main and mizen) and a bowsprit; what is more these three masts must be made up of a lower-mast, topmast and topgallantmast, and anything with only two masts (such as a brig) or with

This is a first-rate, the *Victory* herself, of 100 guns: the upper- and middle-deck gun-ports are open, but as there is a fairly heavy sea running, those on the lower-deck are shut. She is close-hauled on the larboard tack, under courses and topsails; and she is wearing a red ensign because she belongs to a squadron commanded by an admiral of the red.

three all in one piece (such as a polacre) that presumed to call itself a ship would have been laughed to scorn, hooted down, given no countenance whatsoever.

The most usual line-of-battle ship was the 74: there were 73 of them at the beginning of the war and 137 in 1816. A 74 weighed about 1,700 tons and she needed some 2,000 oak trees to build her—57 acres of forest. In the 1790s England could supply much of the wood, but as the years went by the forests began to look very thin, for an oak tree does not spring up overnight; and at least half the timber had to be imported. It was always oak, the very best oak, for nothing else would bear the terrible strain of the winter storms or the shock of battle: fir was tried for frigates and cedar for smaller craft, but it did not answer—heart of oak was the only thing for a man-of-war. Masts and yards had to be imported too: they were made of fir, and they had to be very long and straight. The mainmast of a first-rate was made up of three sections 117, 70 and 35 feet long, while her main yard was 102 feet across—such trees could be found in large numbers only in America or the north.

The building of a man-of-war was a highly-skilled, long and complicated business that I could not describe in less than ten volumes, but roughly this is how they set about it. First the ship was worked out on paper, sometimes following the plans of the beautiful and fast-sailing French or Spanish ships that were captured; then a model might be made, usually to the scale of a quarter of an inch to the foot (there are a great many of these models in the Maritime Museum at Greenwich and several in the London Science Museum); and then the keel would be laid, generally in one of the royal dockyards but sometimes in private shipbuilders' yards. The keel was a massive assembly of elm, and to this were fixed the great rib-like oak timbers, first the stem (in front) and then the stern-post to take the rudder; then came the midship floor-timber and all the rest of the ship's framework. When this was done the ribs were planked inside and out and the beams laid across. The decks were laid on the beams, with proper places for the masts, and when the hull was finished it was divided up by bulkheads into store-rooms, powder-magazines, cabins and so on, with ladders for going up and down, and the whole of the hull that was to be under water was coppered against the attacks of the teredo, a sea-worm that used to pierce holes right through the bottom, before this plating was thought of half way through the eighteenth century.

All this took a long time—the *Victory,* for example, was laid down in 1759 but not launched until 1765—and seeing that the wood was out in all weathers it often began to rot even before the ship was finished. The truth of the matter is that most of the British ships were not nearly so well built as the French or Spanish: they were often slow; they nearly always carried too many guns; they were sometimes very crank—that is, they leaned over in a wind so that they could not open the lower gun-port or the sea would rush in; and occasionally they fell to pieces in a storm. Among the worst were the Forty Thieves, forty ships of the line that were all built in private yards by dishonest contractors, and that were looked upon as floating coffins: but sometimes the royal yards were not much better. Nevertheless the Royal Navy won all the great fleet battles and nearly all the smaller actions between ships of roughly equal force. They did so partly out of force of habit, partly by better gunnery, and even more by better seamanship—you can only learn to be a sailor at sea, and the English Navy was at sea all the year round, whatever the weather, whereas the French and Spaniards were shut up in their harbours.

Now I will say something about the decks, and the sails and rigging, although the pictures show these things better than any number of words. Suppose we were transported to the bottom of a three-decker: we should be in the hold, a vast dark space about 150 feet long, 50 wide and 20 high, with curving sides, with a good many rats in it and a horrible smell of bilge-water—no fresh air and no light, because it would be well under the water-line. Most of it would be taken up with ballast, fresh water in casks, casks of salt pork and beef—enough to feed eight hundred men for six months—the cloth-lined powder magazine, the tin-lined bread-room, and all sorts of other stores. Overhead would be the orlop-deck, near the water-line. Right aft on the orlop was the cockpit, where the older midshipmen lived and where the wounded

A first-rate ship, the *Victory* in cross-section.

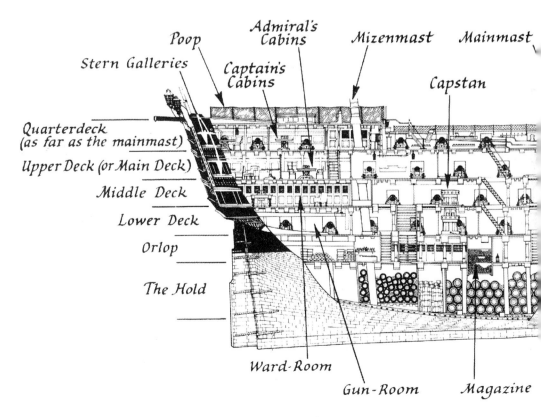

Poop

Stern Galleries

Admiral's Cabins

Captain's Cabins

Mizenmast

Mainmast

Capstan

Quarterdeck (as far as the mainmast)

Upper Deck (or Main Deck)

Middle Deck

Lower Deck

Orlop

The Hold

Ward-Room

Gun-Room

Magazine

were treated in battle; forward of the cockpit were cabins for the junior officers—little dark, airless cupboards; then the sail-room with the spare sails; then the cable-tiers, where the great cables were stowed (some were 25 inches round, and all were 101 fathoms long); then the fore-cockpit where the boatswain and carpenter had their cabins and store rooms. Above the orlop was the lower deck, where the first and heaviest tier of guns stood in two rows facing their gun-ports, 32-pounders, weighing nearly three tons apiece. This was also called the mess-deck, for here the seamen ate and slept. Right aft lay the gun-room, where the gunner lived and where the junior midshipmen slung their hammocks; and right forward was the manger, a compartment designed to prevent the water that came through the hawse-holes from

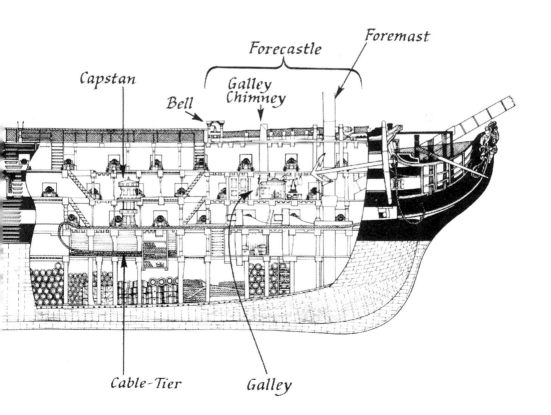

sweeping along the deck—it was also the place where the ship's pigs, sheep and cattle were kept. Above the lower deck came the middle deck, with its rows of 24-pounders; and above that the upper or main deck, with its 18-pounders. The ward-room, where the senior officers messed, was at the after end, and their cabins usually opened off it. Still higher, from the stern to the mainmast, ran the quarterdeck, and on the same level as the quarterdeck, from the fore-shrouds to the bows, the forecastle, the one with ten 12-pounders and the other with two: the quarterdeck and forecastle were connected by gangways. Lastly, above the after part of the quarterdeck, from the mizenmast to the stern, there was the poop, the roof of the captain's quarters—his sleeping cabin, his fore-cabin, and his beautiful great after-cabin which opened on to a stern-gallery (very like a balcony) where he could walk and admire the view in privacy.

But here we are speaking of a first-rate, a three-decker, and many three-deckers were flagships—that is, they had an admiral aboard. When this was so, the great man occupied the after end of the main deck, just under the captain, and the lieutenants and their ward-room moved down to the middle deck.

In the case of two-deckers, the arrangement was much the same, only the middle deck was left out; but in one-deckers, such as frigates, there was no poop—the captain's cabin was under the quarterdeck, on the main deck, and the lieutenants took over the gun-room on the deck below for their mess, banishing the gunner to a cabin forward and the younger midshipmen to the cockpit.

Now for the sails and the rigging. A square-rigged ship had three masts, of course, and these masts were held up by shrouds on each side, by stays to keep them from pitching backwards, and by back-stays to keep them from pitching

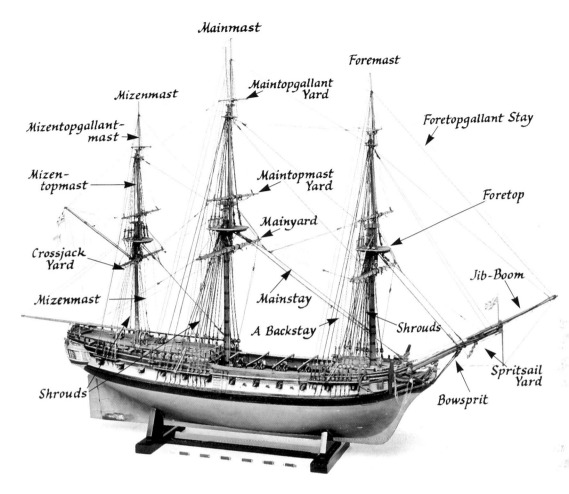

Mainmast

Foremast

Maintopgallant
Yard

Foretopgallant Stay

Mizenmast

Mizentopgallant-
mast

Mizen-
topmast

Maintopmast
Yard

Foretop

Mainyard

Crossjack
Yard

Jib-Boom

Mizenmast

Mainstay

A Backstay

Shrouds

Spritsail
Yard

Shrouds

Bowsprit

Masts, yards and rigging on a 28-gun frigate.

forward: the shrouds had ratlines across them, to make ladders up which the seamen could climb to reach the upper rigging and the sails; and the first set of shrouds led to the platform called the top, or fighting-top, which stood at the junction of the lower-mast and topmast and which served to spread the shrouds for the next section of mast—these masts, by the way, were made to slide up and down through the top, so that in an emergency the topgallantmasts and even topmasts could be struck down on deck. The masts had yards

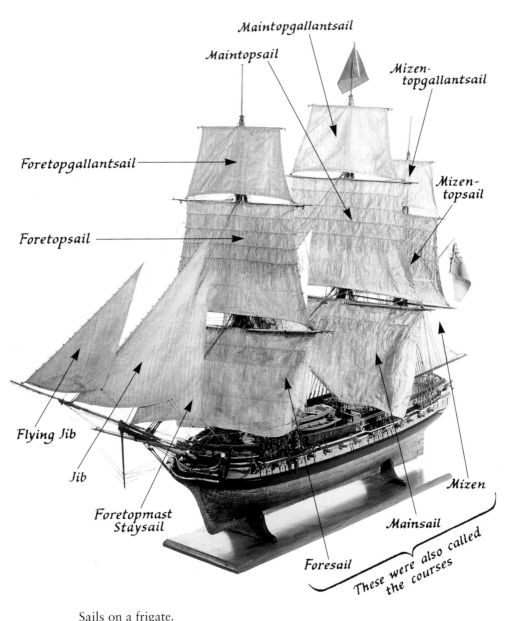

Maintopgallantsail

Maintopsail

Mizen-
topgallantsail

Foretopgallantsail

Mizen-
topsail

Foretopsail

Flying Jib

Jib

Foretopmast
Staysail

Mizen

Mainsail

Foresail

These were also called
the courses

Sails on a frigate.

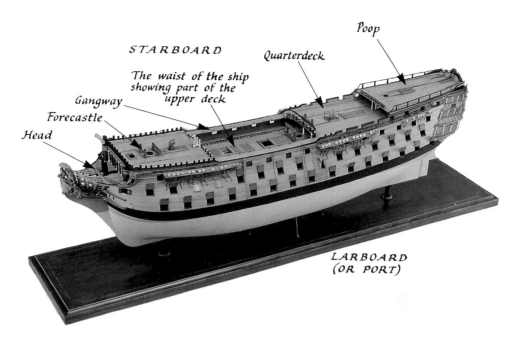

STARBOARD

Poop

Quarterdeck

The waist of the ship
showing part of the
upper deck

Gangway

Forecastle

Head

LARBOARD
(OR PORT)

A two-decker with her bowsprit and masts out and her deck-planking removed to show the construction.

slung across them horizontally, and it was to these yards that the most important sails were attached. The mainmast had a mainyard for the mainsail, a maintopmast yard for its top-sail, a maintopgallant yard, and above that, in fine weather, a royal yard: the foremast had the same four yards with fore tacked on to their names: the lowest yard on the mizen, however, was called the crossjack, which hardly ever had a sail spread on it, because the chief sail on the mizen was a fore-and-aft sail spread by a gaff or lateen over the poop; the rest of its yards were the same. The bowsprit too had its yards and sails—the spritsail and the spritsail-topsail. There were other sails spread on the stays and various booms, but these were the important ones.

When the wind was from behind and the sails were spread, obviously the ship was pushed forward—not that this was

This picture shows three of the ten 12-pounders on the *Victory*'s quarter-deck. You can see the massive breeching on the nearest gun on the larboard side: however, there was little wind, so the sponger, who is ramming down the charge while the captain of the gun feels for it with his priming-iron, is in no danger of being crushed by the muzzle. The next gun forward is just being fired: you can see the captain's powder-horn in his left hand. The pow-

der-boy, holding the cartridge in its box, has been shot. On the starboard side the reduced crew of the forward gun (there should be seven of them) are heaving the gun with their crows while the captain aims it. There are two more cartridge-boxes lying about on the deck. The men shooting over the tight-packed hammocks on the gangways leading from the quarterdeck to the forecastle are Marines. The sailors, as you see, wear no uniforms.

the best point of sailing, because if the breeze were right astern, the after sails would becalm the rest, whereas if it came from her quarter, or 45° abaft the beam, it would fill them all. But when the wind came from the beam, that is to say sideways, or at right-angles to the ship's length, then the square sails would have been useless unless they could swing round to catch its force. And of course that is what happened: the yards were pulled round with braces and the lower corners of the sails were hauled round too—the sheet on the lower leeward corner was hauled aft and the tack, the rope on the windward lower corner, was hauled forward, so that the sail continued to draw; and seeing that the ship could not be forced sideways through the water it went on going forward, though a little sideways too—this sideways motion was called its leeway. Indeed, even when the wind was more from in front than sideways, the ship could still go on: a square-rigged ship, close-hauled, that is, with her yards braced up sharp to an angle of 20° with the keel, could sail within six points of the wind, or 63° 45′ from it—or in other words, if the wind were coming from the north, she could still sail east-north-east.

So much for the ships: now for the guns.

The
Guns

The early guns had beautiful names like cannon-royal, cannon-serpentine, demi-culverin and falconet, but they had a bewildering variety of shot and charge; and since these weapons, together with basilisks, sakers and murdering-pieces might all be mounted on the same deck, it led to sad confusion in time of battle.

By the eighteenth century there were many fewer kinds, and they were called by the weight of the shot they fired: a first-rate, for example, carried 30 32-pounders on her lower deck, 28 24-pounders on her middle deck, 30 18-pounders on her upper deck, 10 12-pounders on her quarterdeck and 2 on her forecastle, thus firing a broadside of 1,158 lb. Everything was plain and straightforward: each deck had guns, shot, cartridges and wads of the same size; the guns could be supplied from the magazines as fast as the powder-boys could run; and all that remained was to fire them as quickly and accurately as possible.

This was something of a task, however, for the gun was a massive brute, mounted on a wheeled carriage, and it had to be fired from a deck that might be in violent motion. An 18-

pounder, a medium-sized gun, had a barrel nine feet long; it weighed 2,388 lb, and it needed a crew of ten to handle it, for not only did it have to be run in and out, but it had to be kept under rigid control—two tons of metal careering about the deck in a rough sea could kill people and smash through the ship's side.

The crew included the captain of the gun, the second captain, a sponger, a fireman, some boarders and sail-trimmers, and a powder-boy, with perhaps a couple of Marines to help in the heaving. They were used to working together, and in crack ships they handled their monsters with wonderful skill: it was English gunnery rather than English ships that won the great naval battles. Each man had his own particular job, so in the roar of battle there was no need for orders. When a gun was to be fired the port was opened, the tight lashings that held the gun to the side were cast loose, and the tompion (the bung that kept the muzzle water-tight) taken out. The men hooked on the tackles—one to each side to heave the gun up to the port and the train-tackle behind to run it inboard for loading—and they seized the breeching to the knob at the end of the gun. This breeching was a stout rope made fast to ring-bolts in the ship's side, and it was long enough to let the gun recoil.

Now, with the gun run in and held by the breeching and the train-tackle, the sponger took the cartridge, a flannel bag with six pounds of powder in it, from the powder-boy, rammed it down the muzzle until the captain felt it in the breech with the priming-iron that he thrust through the touch-hole and cried "Home!" Then the 18-pound shot went down, followed by a wad, both rammed hard: the men clapped on to the side-tackles and ran the loaded gun up, its muzzle as far out as it would go. The captain stabbed the cartridge with his iron, filled the hole and the pan above it with powder from his horn, and the gun was ready to fire, either by a spark from a flint-lock or by a slow-match, a kind of glowing wick. It was aimed right or left by the crew heaving the carriage with their crowbars and handspikes; and the captain, who aimed the gun, could raise or lower it with a wedge under the breech. But although they could send a ball for well over a mile, these guns were not accurate at a distance and they were usually fired at point-blank range—about four hundred yards—or less: indeed, commanders like Nelson preferred to lay their ships yardarm to yardarm, where there was no possibility of missing, and where their double- or treble-shotted guns could fire right through both sides of the enemy.

At the word "Fire!" the captain stubbed the red end of the match into the powder on the pan, the flash ran through the touch-hole to the cartridge and the whole thing went off with an almighty bang. The shot flew out at 1,200 feet a second, the entire gun leapt backwards with terrible force until it was brought up by the breeching, and the air was filled with dense, acrid smoke. The moment it was inboard the captain stopped the vent, the men at the train-tackle held the gun

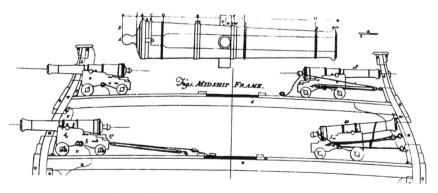

Guns on a man-of-war. The top gun on the right is run in so that it can be loaded; both of those on the left are in the firing position; and the lower one shows the train-tackle. The fourth gun is housed, that is to say made fast so that it cannot move in a heavy sea.

tight, the sponger thrust his wet mop down to clean the barrel and put out any smouldering sparks, another cartridge, shot and wad were rammed home, and the gun was run up again, hard against the port.

It was heavy, dangerous work, above all in action, with the whole broadside firing: the low space 'tween decks would be filled with smoke; little could be seen, little heard, and the slightest false move meant the loss of a leg or an arm from the recoiling gun, to say nothing of the risks of explosion or the enemy's fire. Yet a well-trained crew could carry out the whole operation in one minute forty seconds—three broadsides in just five minutes.

They could do this even in the heat of battle, although some members of the gun-crew had other duties as well. The boarders had their cutlasses ready in their belts and they would leave the gun to batter the enemy by hand at the cry of "Boarders away!" The sail-trimmers would go to their stations when called upon; the fireman had to be ready with his bucket to dash out the first beginnings of a flame aboard; and the second captain to see that the corresponding gun on the other side of the deck was prepared, for few ships had enough people to man two sides at once, and the same crew fought both port and starboard guns.

What they fired was mostly single round shot—the ordinary cannon-ball—and a 32-pounder could smash through two feet of solid oak at half a mile; but at close range they also used grape (a great many small balls in a canvas bag that burst when it was fired, scattering the balls over the enemy's deck and discouraging his crew), canister (much the same), and bar or chain shot to cut up his rigging.

Right through the eighteenth century the Navy used these guns with little change: the 42-pounders were laid aside as being too heavy for even a first-rate (the *Britannia,* or Old

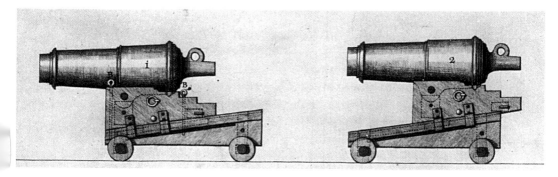

Carronade. These ugly, stumpy little weapons (the 24-pounder was only a yard long) were never counted as real guns, but they did terrible execution at close quarters, they took little room, and they could be handled by many fewer men than the long cannon. In this particular model the carronade recoils up an inclined plane, which diminishes the force: the ordinary kind worked on a horizontal slide, as you see on page 70.

Ironsides as she was called from her massive timbers, was the last to keep them), and the 32-, 24-, 18-, 12-, 9-, 6-, 4- and 3-pounders were the usual armament. Then in 1779 the carronade or smasher was invented: this was a much lighter, shorter gun mounted on slides and designed for close-range fighting. It threw an enormous ball for its weight.

The first ship to be entirely armed with them, by way of experiment, was the *Rainbow,* an old 44. Before this she had carried 20 ordinary 18-pounder long guns on her lower deck, 22 12-pounders on her main deck, and two 6-pounders on her forecastle—a broadside weight of metal of 318 lb, needing about 100 lb of powder to fire it. Now she had 20 68-pounder carronades on her lower-deck, 22 42-pounders on her main-deck, four 32-pounders on her quarterdeck and two on her forecastle—a broadside of 1,238 lb, still needing only about 100 lb of powder, since the charge of the carronade was one twelfth of the weight of its ball, as opposed to the long gun's one third.

The *Rainbow* put to sea, and after six months she found an enemy of the right size—the powerful French 40-gun frigate *Hébé*. The action began in fine style, but to the *Rainbow*'s intense irritation it stopped almost at once. The French captain, seeing these horrible great 32-pound balls coming from the Englishman's forecastle, rightly assumed that there was even worse in store, and struck his colours.

By now it was 1782; the war was almost over and it was too late to try out the carronade in earnest. But by 1793, when the next war began, the Navy was well stocked with them, and they did splendid service in the years to come. They did not replace the long guns, however, most of the carronades being 18- or 12-pounders on the forecastle, quarterdeck and poop. Curiously enough, they were never counted in with the rest of the ship's armament, a 24-gun ship like the

Table showing the size and weight of long guns and carronades

long guns			carronades		
32-pounder	9 feet 6 inches	55 cwt 21 lb	68-pounder	5 feet 2 inches	36 cwt
24-pounder	9 feet 6 inches	50 wt 21 lb	32-pounder	4 feet $\frac{1}{2}$ inch	17 cwt 14 lb
18-pounder	9 feet	42 cwt 21 lb	24-pounder	3 feet	11 cwt 2 qr 25 lb
12-pounder	9 feet	34 cwt 31 lb	18-pounder	2 feet 4 inches	8 cwt 1 qr 25 lb
12-pounder			12-pounder	2 feet 2 inches	5 cwt 3 qr 2 lb
short	7 feet	21 cwt			

Table showing the range of guns and carronades

	32-pounder carronade	24-pounder
point-blank	330 yards	300
5° elevation	1087 yards	1050

(the charge being one twelfth of the weight of the ball in all cases)

32, 24 and 18-pounder long guns

elevation	proportion of powder		to first graze (that is to say, where the ball first touched the water)
2°	$\frac{1}{3}$	single shot	1200 yards
2°	$\frac{1}{4}$	single shot	1000 yards
2°	$\frac{1}{4}$	two shot	500 yards
4°	$\frac{1}{3}$	single shot	1600 yards
7°	$\frac{1}{8}$	single shot	2150 yards
7°	$\frac{1}{4}$	single shot	2020 yards
4°	$\frac{1}{4}$	grape	1000 yards

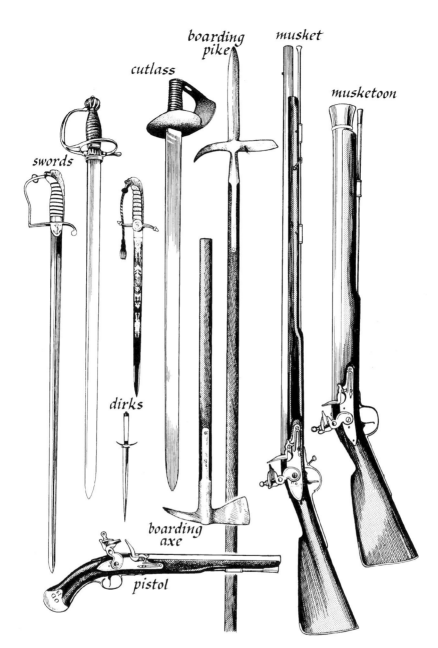

From the man-of-war's armoury, a selection of weapons.

Hyaena, which mounted ten 12-pounder carronades as well as her long guns, remaining a 24-gun ship for official purposes. Firing point-blank meant firing with the gun level: to make the ball go farther one would raise the muzzle, giving it so many degrees of elevation. But point-blank was the most accurate way of firing. When a ball hit the water it would often go skipping over the surface in great bounds: the first impact, however, was by far the most deadly.

The great guns were the man-of-war's chief armament, of course; but they were not the only weapon aboard, by any means. She also carried muskets, for the use of the Marines and the small-arms men in the fighting-tops, pistols, axes and cutlasses for boarding, stinkballs (made of pitch, resin, brimstone, gunpowder and asafoetida in an earthenware pot: it was set on fire and thrown so as to burst among the enemy and overwhelm him with the stench), and grenades for tossing on to the enemy's deck, and boarding-pikes to repel him if he tried to come over the side. We might even add soot to the list, since Lord Cochrane, setting about the 32-gun frigate *El Gamo* with his 14-gun brig *Speedy* in 1803, made his men black their faces in the galley before boarding, to the unspeakable dismay of the Spaniards, who yielded less to the *Speedy*'s little 4-pounders than to the truly hideous appearance of her crew.

The Ship's Company

Now for the men who sailed the ships and fought the guns, and first the officers. Let us take a boy who wants to go to sea and follow him through his career as an officer from bottom to top; and let him be a courageous boy with a cast-iron digestion and lucky enough not to put his head in the way of a cannon-ball, so that he may stay the course. He is a typical boy of quite good family—probably a sea-officer's son or, like Nelson and Jane Austen's brothers, a parson's—but he is not highly educated, since he goes to sea when he is twelve or fourteen, and he has not had much time for school. (Officially the earliest age was eleven for officers' sons and thirteen for the rest, but no one took much notice of the regulation—seven-year-olds were not unknown.) Before he can go to sea his people have to find some captain who is willing to take him aboard, for this is almost the only way to become an officer. They succeed, and the young hero joins his ship with his sea-chest: it is filled to over-flowing, since the captain has not only insisted on the boy's parents giving him an allowance of as much as £50 a year if it is anything like a

Meet Master William Blockhead, who has just been appointed to HMS *Hellfire* on the West Indies station. The young gentleman has probably never been to sea before, or he would not be so pleased with his new dirk; nor would he be carrying a pair of skates to the tropics. The fan-shaped case in front of his sea-chest holds his cocked hat, and on the right of the picture you can see his round hat, with the cockade in it, for every-day wear. The smaller boxes contain preserved meat, green tea, and portable soup (which was dried in slabs, and looked like glue). His medicines include Epsom salts, Friar's Balsam and James's powders; he also has a parcel labelled Rags for Wounds, but in the West Indies he is far more likely to die of yellow jack, a tropical fever that sometimes swept off half a ship's company in a fortnight, than the enemy's violence. On his collar there is a white patch, and if you look at a midshipman today you will see that the white patch is still there.

crack ship, but he will also have sent them a list of necessities. Here is a moderate example:

1 uniform coat superfine cloth
1 uniform coat second best
1 round jacket suit
1 surtout coat and watch-coat

3 pairs of white jean trowsers and waistcoats

3 pairs of nankeen ditto and 3 kerseymere waistcoats

2 round hats with gold loop and cockade

1 glazed hat, hanger (or dirk) and belt

18 linen shirts, frilled

12 plain calico shirts

3 black silk handkerchiefs

12 pocket cotton ditto

12 pairs of brown cotton stockings

6 pairs of white cotton stockings

6 pairs worsted or lamb's wool stockings

2 strong pairs of shoes and 2 light pairs

6 towels and 3 pairs of sheets and pillow-cases

2 table-cloths about 3 yards long

A mattress, 3 blankets and a coverlet

A set of combs and clothes-brushes

A set of tooth-brushes and tooth-powder

A set of shoe-brushes and 12 cakes of blacking or 1/2 doz. bottles of ditto

A pewter wash-hand basin and a pewter cup

A strong sea-chest with a till and 2 trays in it, and a good lock with 2 keys

A quadrant and a small day and night glass

A silver table-spoon and tea-spoon

A knife and fork, and a pocket-knife and penknife

A log-book and journal with paper, pens and ink

Robinson's *Elements of Navigation*

The Requisite Tables and Nautical Almanac

Bible, prayer-book

When going on a foreign station, an additional dress-suit, with more light waistcoats, a cocked hat, and some additional linen.

He reports his presence to the officer of the watch and he is taken to the midshipmen's berth: this is likely to be some-

Midshipman mastheaded: he has lashed himself to the topgallant crosstrees with a handkerchief to prevent himself being blown off while he takes a nap. In fine weather this was not a particularly severe punishment, and an admiral has said that he did most of his reading at the masthead when he was a boy.

thing of a shock to him, since it is a dank, smelly, cheerless hole with no light or air and precious little in the way of food or comfort, very far down in the ship. The midshipmen's berth: but he is not a midshipman—far from it. He is rated first-class volunteer if there is room for one on the ship's books, or captain's servant or even able seaman if there is not, and he will not become a real midshipman for a couple of years. But he does not black the captain's boots, of course, nor attempt an able seaman's duties; he and all like him are called "the young gentlemen" and he wears a midshipman's uniform (blue coat with a white patch on the collar, white breeches and cocked hat for formal occasions, otherwise blue jacket with blue or white trousers and a top hat, and a sword or dirk). Above all, he walks the quarterdeck, the officers' preserve. He has to walk it for six years, learning his duty aloft and on deck, going to the ship's schoolmaster in the mornings for mathematics and navigation, and keeping his official journal; and all this time, whether he is captain's servant, midshipman or master's mate (a senior midshipman) he is in fact only a rating, liable to be disrated at his captain's pleasure or even turned ashore; and if he behaves badly he can be punished, often being sent to the masthead like the young gentleman in the picture, to spend several hours there, repenting of his sins.

At the end of his six years at sea he goes to the Navy Office, bearing certificates of competence and good behaviour from his captains, his journals, and perhaps a paper to say he is twenty. In theory this was the minimum age for a lieutenant, but in fact there were some of fifteen and sixteen. Six years on the ship's books, two of them as a midshipman, was insisted upon, however.

So here he is at the Navy Office with a trembling heart, trying to remember the difference between port and starboard; and here they put him through an oral examination in seamanship and navigation. He is not a booby: he has learnt a good deal in his six years afloat; and he gets through. He has "passed for lieutenant"! He is charmed, delighted, but still very anxious; for it is one thing to pass and quite another to be given the precious commission. However, he has done well at sea, his captains speak well of him, his family has some influence in politics or at the Admiralty, and one day there arrives a beautiful piece of paper covered with official seals and signatures, reading

By the Commissioners for executing the Office of Lord High Admiral of Great Britain and Ireland &c and of all His Majesty's Plantations &c

To Lieutenant William Blockhead, hereby appointed Lieutenant of His Majesty's Ship the Thunderer

By Virtue of the Power and Authority to us given We do hereby constitute and appoint you Lieutenant of His Majesty's Ship the Thunderer, willing and requiring you forthwith to go on board . . . Strictly charging and Commanding all the Officers and Company belonging to the said Thunderer subordinate to you to behave themselves jointly and severally . . . with all due Respect and Obedience . . . And you shall likewise to observe and execute . . . what orders and directions . . . you shall receive from your Captain or any other your superior Officers . . . Hereof nor you nor any of you may fail as you will answer the contrary at your peril.

Now he is a real officer at last, with the King's commission. He comes down on his poor father for a splendid new uniform (a blue coat with white cuffs and white lapels reaching right down his front, white waistcoat and breeches for full dress to be worn on grand occasions, and a plainer blue coat, often worn with trousers or blue breeches, for ordinary wear). He hopes this will be the last time he will have to do so, for now he is earning no less than £5 12s 0d a month, and there is always the golden prospect of prize-money. His father hopes so too.

He joins the *Thunderer,* 74, his commission is solemnly read out to the ship's company, and he takes up his quarters in the ward-room, together with the other lieutenants, the Marine officers, the master, the surgeon, the chaplain and the

This is the famous Captain Bentinck, the prodigious seaman who invented triangular courses, the Bentinck-boom and Bentinck-shrouds. He is in his cabin, asking his son a question about the rigging of the bowsprit on the model under his arm. The boy eventually became a post-captain too, commanding the 38-gun frigate *Phaëton* in her furious set-to with a French 74 on the Glorious First of June, in 1794. Very powerful eyes will make out a disreputable brown spaniel on the left, perfectly at home next to a dismounted block.

purser; it is a handsom room in a 74, with plenty of air and light coming through the great stern window, and he even has a tiny cabin of his own. He forswears the squalor of the midshipmen's berth for ever and settles down to his new duties. The years go by; and usually he moves from ship to ship, gaining a great deal of experience. He becomes more

Passed lieutenant. Here he is in the glory of his lieutenant's uniform. Officers' uniforms changed from time to time, and after 1812 lieutenants were allowed to wear one epaulette. Before that time only the higher ranks had them.

and more senior on the lieutenants' list as his elders are killed or promoted, and in time he is first lieutenant, no longer keeping a watch but responsible for the day-to-day running of the ship, her discipline and her appearance. He draws no extra pay, but he is next in line for promotion, and at last it comes—his ship distinguishes herself in battle and her first lieutenant is made master and commander. He leaves the *Thunderer* after a last splendid party, buys another uniform (a blue gold-laced coat and white breeches for full dress, the same coat and blue breeches for undress) and waits to be given a command of his own. This is another anxious period, for he knows very well that there are about four hundred commanders on the Navy List and no more than about a hundred sloops, the only vessels they can command.

And now, while he is waiting, stirring up all his friends to use their influence, I will say something about uniforms. It is a very curious fact, but before 1748 the Royal Navy had none at all: the officers wore what they thought fit—often red coats, sometimes old tweed breeches at sea, and any kind of hat that caught their fancy. Then in that year uniform was laid down for the officers, but it was not until 1857 that the men had one—they fought the Battle of Trafalgar in anything from petticoat breeches (a kind of depraved kilt dating from the middle ages) to canvas trousers, with fur caps, top hats or handkerchiefs on their heads, and jerseys or chequered shirts; though most wore the purser's slops, which were roughly of a pattern. But although he had no uniform, the man-of-war's man could be recognized at once, particularly when he was in his shore-going rig: this usually consisted of a shiny black glazed tarpaulin hat (hence Jack Tar for a sailor) with a long dangling ribbon embroidered with the name of his ship, a bright blue jacket with gilt buttons down the right side, very broad, loose trousers, white or blue, tiny black shoes with bows or silver buckles, a shirt, white, spotted, striped or coloured, open at the collar, and black silk hand kerchief loosely knotted round the neck, and a long scarlet waistcoat, the whole decorated with ribbons at the seams, for glory. As well as this he often had little gold earrings and a long swinging pigtail (those whose hair did not grow would sometimes eke it out with oakum), so that there was no mistaking the man-of-war's man, particularly as he chewed his tobacco rather than smoking it like a Christian. I will also say something about sloops. Rightly speaking, a sloop is and always was a one-masted fore-and-aft vessel; but the Admiralty extended the term to cover ships and other craft that could be commanded by a master and commander, so that when a man-of-war brig had a lieutenant as her captain she

During the Battle of St Vincent, which was fought on St Valentine's Day 1797, Nelson, in the *Captain*, 74, boarded the *San Nicolas*, a Spanish 80-gun ship, took her, hurried across her deck to the even bigger *San Josef*, an enormous three-decker of 112 guns, and took her too (see page 76). Here he is on the quarterdeck of the Spanish first-rate, receiving the dying admiral's sword. To his right, by the Spanish chaplain (who has certainly been absolving the dying) there is a dismounted gun: to his left stands Captain Berry, recently promoted master and commander, as you

may see by the single epaulette on his left shoulder; and next to Captain Berry there is an English seaman called Hopper, who struck the Spanish colours and who is now tidily bundling them up. Behind him there is the wheel, and above that the *San Josef*'s bell, which now hangs in HMS *Ganges*, the Navy's training establishment in Suffolk. At this time Nelson was a commodore (a captain in command of a squadron), but commodores had the right to a rear-admiral's uniform, which he wears here.

Michael Seymour was one of the great fighting frigate captains. He was a parson's son from Ireland: he joined the Navy at 12, was promoted lieutenant at 22, lost an arm two years later in the battle of the Glorious First of June, in 1794, was made master and commander in 1795 and post-captain in 1800, when he was 32. He had several temporary commands, but then in 1806 he was given the *Amethyst,* a fine 32-gun frigate. In 1808 he took the *Thétis,* a French frigate of greater force, and for this he was given the Naval Medal, a rare distinction in those days (see page 81). Then the next year he took the even heavier *Niémen,* and he was made a baronet. He died a rear-admiral, but here he is a post-captain, wearing the two epaulettes of a captain with three years' seniority: his empty sleeve is pinned to his coat, and above it there is the medal

was a brig (with two masts), but the moment a commander took her over she became a mere sloop, to the unspeakable amazement of landsmen.

Our young commander was born lucky. He has his sloop in a month or two—she takes a French corvette of equal force and he is promoted again. He is posted into a frigate, for he is now a post-captain. As a commander he was called Captain Blockhead by courtesy, and of course he was the captain of his ship; but now he is a full-blown captain and he is so addressed in official letters by the Admiralty.

Admiral of the Fleet Earl St Vincent, wearing the red ribbon and the star of the Order of the Bath. Around his neck he wears the St Vincent medal for the battle he won, with Nelson's help, on St Valentine's day in 1797 and from which he took his title. He was a rigid disciplinarian, and in the service they called him "Old Jarvie" (his family name was Jervis), rather as they might have said "Old Nick".

Here is the leonine Admiral Holburne, in all the glory of full dress. He saw a great deal of service, particularly in the Seven Years War: once, when he was blockading the French in Louisburg (the gateway to Canada) a most appalling storm blew up; it reached hurricane-force during the night, and when at last it died away the Admiral found that thirteen of his twenty-three ships had lost some or all of their masts, one had been wrecked, one was on the rocks, and one had foundered with all hands. However, the Admiral survived this, as he survived much else, and in time he became a Lord of the Admiralty and Governor of Greenwich Hospital. His son, the very young gentleman at his side, shows an early example of the midshipman's white patches: in the ordinary course of a naval career, particularly with such a father, he should have been a post-captain by Nelson's time, but I can find no trace of him. He may well have been devoured by sharks while still so tender

This time he does not have to buy a new uniform: his old coat will do, and all that is needed is to shift his epaulette from his left shoulder to his right, with the comforting reflection (if his promotion is before 1812) that when he is a captain of three years' seniority he will wear two, one on each shoulder, and the even more comforting reflection that from now on his promotion is automatic.

Many of his former shipmates have stuck at lieutenant, many at commander, but the post-captains move steadily up the list, and now nothing but death or very shocking misconduct will prevent him from being an admiral at last. After some years in frigates he is given a ship of the line, and slowly he climbs the captains' list until at last he is at the top. The oldest of all the full admirals dies, and everyone moves up a step—our post-captain is made a rear-admiral! There is one

Ward-room. This picture was painted by the Rev. Edward Mangin, a parson who spent a few months aboard HMS *Gloucester* as a naval chaplain. The *Gloucester* was a 74, and she carried twelve ward-room officers: five lieutenants, three Royal Marine officers, the master, the surgeon, the purser and the chaplain. They are all here at table, each with his servant behind his chair, a ship's boy or a Marine private. The small cabins on each side, where the officers sleep, are all swept away when the ship is cleared for action, because the aftermost guns are there, as well as the officers' cots.

The ship's purser, by Rowlandson.

last anxiety in his mind, however: he may be given no flag—
he may be only a "yellow admiral", condemned to live the
rest of his life ashore on half-pay. But his luck still holds, and
not only is he made rear-admiral of the blue but he is given a
squadron to command. He goes aboard his flagship, hoists
his blue ensign at the mizen; the squadron salutes it with thirteen guns and they proceed to sea. (The Navy never *goes:* it
always *proceeds*.) But however well he fights it makes no difference to his promotion. He moves up the flaglist automati-

Tom Allen, an example of the best kind of seaman. He was Nelson's coxswain and if there had not been many more like him in the fleet, Nelson would never have won his famous victories.

cally—no one can get ahead of him and he cannot get ahead of anyone else, no matter what victories he may win. Rear-admiral of the blue, of the white, of the red. (In the seventeenth century, when very numerous fleets were engaged in the Dutch wars, the British fleets were divided into three squadrons, the red in the centre, the white in the van and the blue in the rear; and each squadron had its own admiral, vice-admiral and rear-admiral, the admiral of the red squadron being the admiral of the fleet.) Then vice-admiral of the blue, the white, hoisting his white ensign at the fore (this was the highest rank that Nelson ever reached), and of the red. Then admiral, full admiral: and at last, an old, old, very old man, he hoists the union flag at the main, for he is the most senior of them all, the admiral of the fleet.

I have spoken of other officers in the ward-room, the master, the surgeon and the purser: they messed in the ward-room and they had the right to walk the quarterdeck, but they were not commissioned officers—they held a warrant from the Navy Office and they never had quite the standing of the others. The master was a relic from the times when sailors sailed the ships and soldiers did the fighting, and he was still responsible for the navigation; he usually began as a midshipman, became a master's mate, and then, having few social advantages and no influence, gave up all hope of a commission, accepted a warrant and so reached the highest rank that he was ever likely to attain. The surgeon was the ship's medical man, of course; and the purser looked after the ship's provisions and the slops, or clothes that were sold to the men at sea; he had almost nothing to do with pay. The purser was not often a popular officer, and "pusser's tricks" meant any kind of swindle with food, drink, tobacco and clothes, the most notorious being "purser's eights", or his habit of receiving food at sixteen ounces to the pound and serving it out at fourteen, keeping the odd two for himself.

There were other warrant officers, such as the boatswain, who looked after the rigging, sails, anchors, cables and cordage, and who hurried the men to their duty, and the gunner and the carpenter, who were of great importance in the life of the ship: they usually rose from the lower deck, and they messed by themselves, not in the ward-room.

The lower deck itself was made up of the great mass of the ship's people—all the ratings from boy, third class (the lowest form of marine life) to able seaman. The captain appointed the petty officers such as the quartermasters, ship's corporal, boatswain's mate and so on from among them, but it made little difference to their sense of being the same kind of men. They nearly all lived and messed together on the lower deck between the guns, slinging their hammocks from the low beams overhead. They were allowed fourteen inches a man, but as they were divided into two watches, larboard and starboard, each on duty in turn, they usually had the luxury of twenty-eight inches to lie in: some 500 men packed into a space about 150 feet long and 50 at the widest. Their life was very hard, often dangerous, and always ill-paid; what is more, their meagre pay was invariably kept six months in arrears, in the hope that this would prevent them from running away. If their food had been good in the first place and if it had been honestly served out and decently cooked, it would not have been too bad by the standards of the time; but generally this was not the case. Indeed, it was usually so bad that when they could catch them, the men often ate rats, or millers as they were called in the service, because of their dusty coats as they got into the flour and dried peas. They were neatly skinned and cleaned and laid out for sale: hungry midshipmen would buy them too, and Admiral Raigersfeld, looking back on his youth, says, "They were full as good as rabbits, although not so large." Speaking of the bread he observes, "The biscuit that was served to the ship's company was so light, that when you tipped it upon the table, it almost fell into dust, and thereout numerous insects, called weevils, crawled; they were bitter to the taste, and a sure indication that the biscuit had lost its nutritious particles; if instead of these weevils, large white maggots with black heads made their appearance (these were called bargemen in the Navy), then the biscuit was considered to be only in its first state of decay; these maggots were fat and cold to the taste, but not bitter."

Here is a list of the provisions that were usually served out:

Sunday, 1 lb of biscuit, 1 lb of salt pork, half a pint of dried peas.

Monday, 1 lb of biscuit, half a pint of oatmeal, 2 oz of sugar and butter, 4 oz of cheese.

Tuesday, 1 lb of biscuit, 2 lb of salt beef.

Wednesday, 1 lb of biscuit, half a pint of peas and oatmeal, 2 oz of butter and sugar.

Thursday, 1 lb of biscuit, 1 lb of pork, half a pint of peas, 4 oz of cheese.

Friday, 1 lb of biscuit, half a pint of peas and oatmeal, sugar, butter and cheese as before.

Saturday, 1 lb of biscuit and 2 lb of beef.

When beer was to be had, they were given a gallon a day; when it was not, which was most of the time, they had their beloved grog. This was rum, mixed with three times the amount of water and a little lemon-juice against scurvy: they were given a pint of grog at dinner time and another for supper, and they often got dead drunk, particularly when they saved up their rations and drank it all at once.

They were nearly always uneducated, often unable to read or write, and they had generally lived very hard all their lives; but there were some wonderful men among them, brave, very highly skilled at their calling, magnificently loyal to their shipmates and to their officers if they were well led. As Nelson said, "Aft the more honour, forward the better man." By aft he meant the quarterdeck, abaft the mainmast, the officers' part of the ship, and by forward he meant the men, the foremast jacks, who lived forward of the mainmast.

They were brought together partly by free entry (popular officers like Saumarez or Cochrane could always man their ships with volunteers) and partly by the press-gang. Impressment was a rough and ready form of conscription, and the

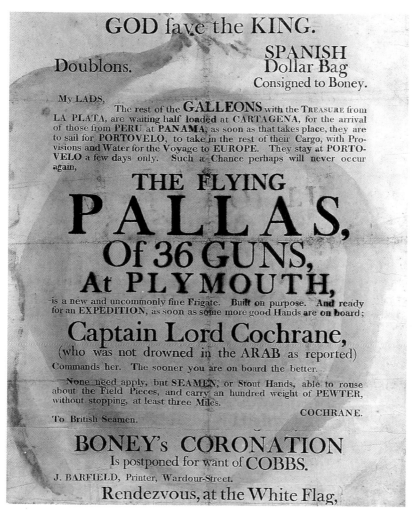

GOD save the KING.

Doublons.

SPANISH
Dollar Bag
Consigned to Boney.

My LADS,
 The rest of the GALLEONS with the TREASURE from LA PLATA, are waiting half loaded at CARTAGENA, for the arrival of those from PERU at PANAMA, as soon as that takes place, they are to sail for PORTOVELO, to take in the rest of their Cargo, with Provisions and Water for the Voyage to EUROPE. They stay at PORTO-VELO a few days only. Such a Chance perhaps will never occur again,

THE FLYING
PALLAS,
Of 36 GUNS,
At PLYMOUTH,

is a new and uncommonly fine Frigate. Built on purpose. And ready for an EXPEDITION, as soon as some more good Hands are on board;

Captain Lord Cochrane,

(who was not drowned in the ARAB as reported)
Commands her. The sooner you are on board the better.

 None need apply, but SEAMEN, or Stout Hands, able to rouse about the Field Pieces, and carry an hundred weight of PEWTER, without stopping, at least three Miles.

COCHRANE.

To British Seamen.

BONEY's CORONATION
Is postponed for want of COBBS.

J. BARFIELD, Printer, Wardour-Street.

Rendezvous, at the White Flag,

Most captains put out handbills and posters of this kind when they were commissioning a ship, in the hope of attracting volunteers; but none except popular and successful officers ever succeeded in getting real men-of-war's men to come forward, and they had to rely on the press-gang.

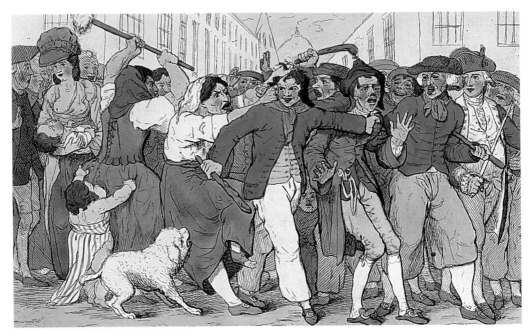

The press-gang. Here a wretched tailor is being pressed. He will not be much use—a dozen spindle-shanked landsmen would not be the equivalent of one able seaman—but he is all the Navy can get, and at least he will be able to haul on a rope. The seaman on his right, the one whose hair is being pulled, wears trousers, a rare garment in those days, and the one on his left petticoat-breeches. The man with a sword is an officer: all gangs were supposed to be commanded by a lieutenant.

idea was that seamen should be taken from merchant ships or seized on land and compelled to serve in the fleet for as long as their services were required. In practice it meant that a short-handed ship (and a man-of-war needed an enormous crew—roughly ten times the size of a merchantman's) would send an officer ashore with a strong party of powerful, reliable sailors armed with pistols and cutlasses for show and clubs for use to catch any reasonably able-bodied man they could lay their hands on—seamen for choice but anyone who could haul on a rope if sailors were not to be found. There was also the impress service itself, where shore-based officers did much the same, sending their prey to receiving ships, whence they were drafted to the men-of-war. Then, in 1795, there was the quota-system, by which each county was required to provide so many men for the Navy. The counties responded by getting rid of their undesirables—thieves, poachers, paupers, general nuisances, nearly all of them landsmen, or as the men-of-war's men called them, grass-combing lubbers.

Faced with recruits of this kind, some of them straight from gaol, many officers tightened the already severe discipline of their ships: flogging became more frequent and more savage, and "starting", hitting people with a cane or a rope's end, to make them jump to their work, grew far worse. The real seamen came in for a good deal of this, and they began to feel even more ill-used, particularly as these alleged volunteers, who were sometimes given the choice between transportation and the Navy, received a bounty of as much as £70—well over four years' pay for an able seaman. The sailors were ill-used, they were knocked about, they were not paid at all when they were sick or wounded and off duty, their pay was always in arrears, they were allowed almost no shore-leave at home, and they were cheated out of their rations. At Spithead in 1797 they mutinied. This was a very important mutiny, not like the small though sometimes bloody outbreaks against a tyrannical brute of a captain: the men refused to take the fleet to sea unless their grievances were put right. They were extraordinarily moderate, merely petitioning the Admiralty, in the most respectful terms, for an increase in pay to bring their nineteen shillings a month up to the soldier's shilling a day, that their pound of provisions should be sixteen ounces, that fresh vegetables, instead of flour, should be served out when they were in port, and that they might be allowed a short leave to visit their families. They said they should certainly take their ships to sea if the French fleet came out; but until then they should stand by their demands. Nelson, among other officers, stated that "his heart was with them" and that he was against "the infernal system" of paying them by ticket rather than cash, so that they often had to leave their families penniless for years. In the end the Admiralty gave way; a bill was hurried through parliament, the mutineers were given the King's pardon, and they carried Lord Howe, the admiral who had conducted the negotiations, shoulder-high through the streets of Portsmouth.

Reefing topsails. The men are out on the yard and they are hauling up the sail to get at the reef-points, the plaited lines flying out from its surface, so as to be able to tie them to the yard, thus reducing the area of the sail. The spar running from the shrouds to the ring at the end of the yard is a studdingsail-boom.

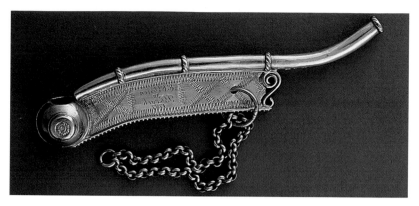

Boatswain's call. These calls were usually made of silver: they were used by the boatswain and his mates to pipe the hands to their various duties—a different call for every manoeuvre—and to welcome important visitors aboard. They made a weird howling noise, surprising to a landsman's ear.

Before giving a table showing the pay of the Navy after these improvements and after some rises for the officers too, I will quickly run through the stations and duties of the crew. The older, most highly skilled able seamen were stationed on the forecastle; they were called sheet-anchor or forecastle-men, and there would be about 45 of them in a 74. Then came the topmen, all able seamen, but young and active, since all the duty above the lower yards fell to them: counting fore, main and mizen topmen, there would be 114 altogether. Then came the afterguard, mostly ordinary seamen and land-men, who worked the after-braces, main, mizen and lower stay sails: they would number about 60. Lowest of all in public esteem were the waisters, a numerous body (115) of land-men and other poor creatures stationed in the waist to look after the main and fore sheets and do all the dirty, unskilled work that was going. Then there were the quartermasters, old, reliable seamen who conned the ship, directing the helmsman; and the quarter-gunners, each of whom had charge of four guns. Last there were the idlers, or people who did not keep a watch but only worked from dawn till eight at night, such as the master-at-arms, the cook, the sailmaker, the barber and so on.

Pay (per lunar month—there are 13 lunar months in a year)

Admiral of the Fleet	140	0	0	
Admiral	98	0	0	
Vice-Admiral	70	0	0	
Rear-Admiral	49	0	0	
Captain (of a first rate)	32	4	0 down to 16 16 0 in a 6th rate
Master and Commander	16	16	0
Lieutenant	8	8	0
Master (1st rate)	12	12	0 down to 7 7 0 in a 6th rate
Boatswain, gunner, purser	4	16	0 down to 3 1 0 in a 6th rate
Carpenter	5	16	0 down to 4 16 0 in a 6th rate
Master's mate	3	16	6 down to 2 12 6 in a 6th rate
Midshipman	2	15	6 down to 2 0 6 in a 6th rate
Chaplain	11	10	$9\frac{1}{4}$ (plus £5 a year from each midshipman and 1st class volunteer, and £20 a year for doing the duty of a schoolmaster)
Able seaman	1	13	6
Ordinary seaman	1	5	6
Landman	1	2	6
Boy (1st class)	9	0	0 a year
Boy (2nd class)	8	0	0 a year
Boy (3rd class)	7	0	0 a year

Armourer, 2.4.3, master-at-arms, 2.0.6, carpenter's mate 2.10.6, caulker and ropemaker 2.10.6, quartermaster and boatswain's mate 2.5.6, sailmaker and cooper 2.5.6 (1st rate) 2.0.6 (6th), gunners' mate 2.2.6, yeoman of the powder-room 2.0.6, caulker's mate 2.6.6, yeoman of the sheets 2.2.6 (1st rate) 1.16.6 (6th rate), captains of the forecastle, tops and afterguard 2.0.6 (1st rate) 1.16.6 (6th).

Life at Sea

Officially the ship's day ran from noon to noon, but to most of those aboard it seemed to begin about dawn or earlier, just before eight bells in the middle watch, or 4 a.m., when the boatswain's mates piped "All hands" down the fore and main hatchways and hurried below roaring "Larboard watch ahoy! Rise and shine. Show a leg there! Out or down, out or down. Rouse out, you sleepers," and cutting down the hammocks of those who preferred to stay in bed, having had no more than four hours of sleep.

The business of the ship, when at sea, had to go on right round the clock, naturally, since she could not be tied up to a post for the night; and to deal with this situation the ship's company was divided into two watches, larboard (or port) and starboard, and the 24 hours were cut into seven periods of duty, also called watches, thus:

Noon to 4 p.m., afternoon watch	8 p.m. to midnight, first watch
4 p.m. to 6 p.m., first dog-watch	midnight to 4 a.m., middle watch
6 p.m. to 8 p.m., last dog-watch	4 a.m. to 8 a.m., morning watch
	8 a.m. to noon, forenoon watch.

The odd number of watches meant that the night duty was fairly shared: the larboard watch would turn out at midnight one day and the starboard the next. But the two-watch system also meant that most of the men never had more than four hours' sleep at a time. The officers were divided into three watches, which gave them longer in bed, but on the other hand they were never allowed to sleep on duty whereas in calm weather the men who were not at the wheel or looking out might drowse in most ships when there was nothing to be done. The passage of time was marked by strokes on the ship's bell, one stroke for every half hour: so eight bells meant the end of the ordinary watch. And at every stroke the log was heaved, the speed of the ship and her course marked on the log-board, and the depth of water in the well reported by the carpenter or one of his mates, while at night all the sentinels called "All's well."

To go back to eight bells in the middle watch: as they were struck, so the watch that had been sleeping, the larboard watch, let us say, was mustered and the watch on duty dismissed to get what sleep they could before hammocks were piped up. About this time the idlers or day-men were called, and at two bells the decks were cleaned, first being wetted, then sprinkled with sand, then scrubbed with holystones great and small, then brushed, and lastly dried with swabs. This took until six bells, and at seven bells hammocks were piped up. Each man took his hammock (it had a number on it, corresponding with the number on the beam where it was slung), rolled it into a tight cylinder and brought it up on deck, where the quartermasters stowed them in the hammock-nettings along the sides: this aired the bedding after the awful fug below, provided some protection in case of battle (a hammock would stop a musketball and deaden a cannon-ball), and cleared the lower deck for cleaning.

At eight bells in the morning watch hands were piped to breakfast, which was biscuit, burgoo (a kind of milkless porridge) and, in some ships, cocoa. Half an hour was allowed for this feast. Now it was the forenoon watch and the starboard men were on duty again (the two watches were often called the larbowlines and starbowlines). The watch below cleaned the lower deck, with water if the weather was fine and the ports could be opened to dry the planks, otherwise with dry sand, holystones and brooms; then they might be allowed to rest, but some captains preferred them to exercise the great guns or to practise reefing topsails.

At eight bells in the forenoon watch the officers took the noon observations of the sun to fix the ship's position, the watch was changed and all hands piped to dinner. The men divided themselves into messes, usually of eight friends, and one of the eight was appointed their cook for the day: he received the mess's ration from the ship's cook in the galley, saw to its dressing and brought it to his messmates as they sat at their hanging table between the guns. It took about half an hour to eat, and then at one bell the fifer on the main deck began to play "Nancy Dawson" or some other tune that meant the grog was ready. The cooks darted up the ladder with little tubs or blackjacks to the butt where the master's mate had publicly mixed the rum, water and lemon-juice. He served it out with great care, and with great care the cooks carried it down, while their messmates banged their plates and cheered. It was shared out, but in tots slightly smaller than the tot the officer had used, so that a little was left over: this was called the cook's plush, and he drank it as a reward for his trouble.

At two bells dinner was over: the larbowlines were on duty, and generally the starbowlines were turned up as well for exercise. At eight bells in the afternoon watch, or 4 p.m.,

The ship's cook. Cooks were generally pensioners from the great naval hospital at Greenwich, and it was rare that any had both arms and both legs.

hands were piped to supper, which was much the same as breakfast, but with another issue of grog. Supper took half an hour; by this time it was one bell in the first dog-watch, and a little later the drum beat to quarters. All hands hurried to their action-stations and the guns were cast loose. The midshipmen and then the lieutenants inspected the men under their charge and eventually the first lieutenant, having received their reports, reported "All present and sober, sir, if you please," to the captain, who would then have the guns run in and out and perhaps fired, or topsails reefed or furled and loosed.

When this was over the drum beat the retreat, hammocks

were piped down, and at eight bells the watch was mustered. The larboard watch went below, straight to sleep; lights were put out on the lower deck, and the starboard watch took up its duty. At eight bells the larbowlines were called again for the middle watch, and four hours later, towards dawn, the day began again with the cleaning of the decks, this time by the starboard watch.

As you see, the men had at the most four hours of sleep one night and seven the next, with what they might snatch during the day. But in any emergency, such as reducing sail in dirty weather or tacking ship, or the least hint of action, all hands would be called and the watch below tumbled up, perhaps with no sleep at all.

This was an ordinary ship's day; but on others the routine changed, particularly on Thursdays and Sundays. On Thursdays hammocks were piped up at 4 a.m.; the hands spent the morning washing their clothes and the afternoon making and mending them. On Sundays hammocks were piped up at six bells and breakfast was at seven bells; then the ship and everything in her was brought to a high state of perfection, the men washed, shaved and put on their clean good clothes; they combed and plaited one another's pigtails, and at five bells in the forenoon watch they were mustered by divisions, the lieutenant of each division inspecting them as they stood in lines, toeing one particular seam on the deck. Then the captain, having inspected them too, went right round the ship with the first lieutenant to see that everything, including the cook's great coppers, was spotless. It usually was, but if he found anything dirty or out of order, then there would be the very devil to pay. After the captain's inspection there was a service on the quarterdeck, conducted by the chaplain if the ship carried one and by the captain if she did not. Some captains would preach a sermon, but others merely read out the Articles of War.

Two lower-deck messes have joined to sing and have fun and drink their grog together. On either side of the hanging table there is a great gun, carefully housed, with its sponge and rammer over it, and a pair of cutlasses. The plates belonging to the mess are against the ship's side, together with the numbered ditty-bags in which the seamen kept their personal belongings.

Then the men were piped to dinner, which might include such delights as figgy-dowdy, made by putting ship's biscuits into a canvas bag, pounding them with a marlinspike, adding bits of fat, figs and raisins, and boiling the whole in a cloth.

George Cruikshank

Until suppertime they were as free as the work of the ship allowed. If they were in company with other ships or in port they would often go ship-visiting; or the liberty-men might be allowed on shore, especially in such places as Malta or Gibraltar, where it was easy to catch them if they tried to desert. After supper they were mustered, each man passing in front of the captain as his name was called and checked off on the ship's books: and when the muster was over it was time for quarters again.

Some ships had special days for punishment; others might punish all round the week. It always took place at six bells in the forenoon watch. The boatswain's mates piped "All hands to witness punishment" and the men flocked aft, where the Marines were drawn up with their muskets on the poop and all the officers were present in formal dress, wearing their swords. The master-at-arms brought his charges before the captain and the misconduct of which they were accused (usually drunkenness) was publicly stated. If the man had anything to say for himself he might do so, and if any of his par-

A man has been accused of a fault and is about to be flogged by the boatswain's mate with a cat-of-nine-tails when the real culprit comes forward with his shirt already off. The captain, his officers and two midshipmen are on the starboard side of the quarterdeck, and the Marines are drawn up on the poop. On the right, abaft the mainmast, you see some of the ship's company. Over to port there are two heavy carronades, with their rammers hanging above, against the bulwark, and over them a neatly stowed line of hammocks.

ticular officers saw fit they might put in a word for him. Having considered the case, the captain gave his decision— acquittal, reprimand or punishment. This might be extra duties or stoppage of grog, but often it was flogging. "Strip," the captain would say, and the seaman's shirt came off. "Seize him up," and the quartermasters tied his hands to a grating rigged for the purpose upright against the break of the poop, reporting, "Seized up, sir." Then the captain read the Articles of War that covered the offence, he and all the others taking off their hats as he did so. He said, "Do your duty," and a boatswain's mate, taking the cat-of-nine-tails out of a red baize bag, laid on the number of strokes awarded. Some hands screamed, but the regular man-of-war's man would take a dozen in silence.

It was a vile, barbarous business by our standards, and an ugly one even by the more brutal standards of the time—no women were allowed to witness it. Many captains, Nelson and Collingwood among them, hated flogging, and there were ships that kept excellent taut discipline without bringing the cat out of the bag for months on end; but there were other captains, such as the infamous Pigot of the *Hermione* whose crew eventually hacked him to pieces off the Spanish Main, who rigged the grating almost every day and whose sentences, instead of Collingwood's six, nine or at the most twelve strokes, actually ran into the hundreds.

These men were despised by their fellow-officers, not only for being inhuman brutes but for being inefficient brutes into the bargain. A happy ship was the only excellent fighting-machine—a ship whose well-trained, well-led crew would follow their officers anywhere, a ship that would fight like a tiger when she came into action.

Action was the goal of every sea-officer; and when it came, how a ship sprang to life! The drum beat to quarters, the men

Negapatam. This battle, between Admiral Hughes with eleven ships of the line and one frigate and Admiral de Suffren with twelve of the line and four heavy frigates, was fought in 1782 off the Coromandel coast, in India. The painter has put the ships too close together to get them all into the picture, but it gives a good idea of the traditional line of battle, with

the frigates lying outside. The two fleets fought from about eleven in the morning until half-past four, but although the English had 300 men killed or wounded and the French at least 779, the battle led to no victory or captures on either side. One of the French captains did strike his colours, but his officers refused to obey him or to give up the ship.

On 1 August 1798 Nelson found the French fleet at anchor in the almost
uncharted and shallow Aboukir Bay not far from the mouth of the Nile.
They expected him to attack from the seaward side, where the water was
deeper, but he sent some of his ships down the inside of their line, con-
centrating his force on the French van and centre and placing the enemy
between two fires. He took, burnt or sank all the French ships of the line
except two at the rear. On the left of the line there are the frigates: only
two of them escaped. The battle began as the sun was setting: in the dark-
ness *L'Orient*, a great French three-decker, took fire, and at about midnight the flames reached her powder-magazines. She blew up with a most
appalling explosion, killing almost every soul aboard.

raced to their familiar stations and cast loose their guns, the officers' cabins disappeared, the thin bulkheads, the furniture and all lumber vanishing into the hold to give a clear sweep fore and aft, the decks were wetted and sanded against fire. Damp cloth screens appeared around the hatches; in the magazines the gunner and his mates served out powder to the boys with their cartridge-cases; the yards were secured with chains, the galley fires were put out; and all this happened in a matter of minutes.

If it was a fleet action the captain and his first lieutenant

St Vincent. This is the kind of free-for-all that developed once the old line
of battle was abandoned. The picture above shows only part of the battle,
in which 15 British and 23 Spanish ships of the line were engaged. At this
point Nelson, in the *Captain*, is boarding the *San Nicolas*, which has fallen
foul of the huge *San Josef*. Having taken the *San Nicolas* he used her as a
bridge to get at the *San Josef* (see page 46). The next picture shows him
slashing away in the waist of the *San Josef*. (He still had his right arm
then: a few months later he lost it in battle.) The Spanish officer on the
left at the quarterdeck rail, raising his hat and presenting his sword, is calling out that the ship surrenders.

Camperdown, 1797. This battle with the Dutch fleet was one of the fiercest engagements in the war. The Dutch fought hard, as they always do, but the English seamen, who had just returned to duty after the mutiny at the Nore, fought harder still; and here is Admiral de Winter surrendering his sword to Admiral Duncan. The two admirals were among the biggest men afloat, and yet, as one remarked to the other, neither had even been scratched by the storm of shot that flew between the ships. On the left there is one of the tubs that held slow-match for the guns; just beyond it a seaman, stripped to the waist, is heaving a gun with a crow or handspike, and to his right an officer is calling up into the shrouds with a speaking-trumpet. Overhead you see the splinter-netting that was rigged to protect the people on deck from falling blocks and lumps of wood; and on the right of the picture there is a dismounted gun.

on the quarterdeck would have their eyes on the admiral or the repeating frigates almost as much as on the enemy, for it was of the first importance to follow the admiral's signals. The traditional fleet action was begun with both sides manoeuvring for the weather-gage—that is, trying to gain a position to windward of the enemy so as to have the advantage of forcing an engagement at the right moment. Then the two fleets would form their line of battle, usually with about four hundred yards between the ships in each line to allow for change of course; and the idea was that each captain should engage his opposite number on the other side. The Fighting Instructions insisted that the battle-line should be rigidly maintained, and any captain who strayed from it was liable to be court-martialled: he must keep his station, and, since those who were not next to the admiral in this straight line could not see his signals because of the sails of the next ahead or astern, they had to watch the frigates (which always lay outside the line) whose duty it was to repeat the flagship's orders.

But these battles rarely led to a decisive result, and in 1782 in the West Indies, Rodney disobeyed the Instructions, broke the French line and captured the enemy flagship and five others. In the war that began in 1793 nearly all the great fleet actions disregarded official tactics. "Never mind manoeuvres," said Nelson. "Always go at them." This he did at Saint Vincent, the Nile and Trafalgar, just as Duncan did at Camperdown: after the first formal approach the fleet action quickly became a wild free-for-all in which better gunnery and seamanship won the day. At St Vincent, for example, Sir John Jervis, with Nelson under his orders and fifteen ships of the line, took on a Spanish fleet of 27, including seven first rates, captured four and beat the rest into a cocked hat.

Another and more frequent sort of action was that fought between frigates, sometimes in small squadrons but more often as single ships; and in these everything depended on the captain—he fought his ship alone. One of the finest was the battle between HMS *Amethyst*, 36, and the French *Thétis*, 40. Late on a November evening in 1808, close in with the

This is the *Amethyst* racing after the *Thétis* through a heavy sea with the lee-shore just at hand. The *Thétis* has her larboard maintopsail and topgallant studdingsails aboard: the *Amethyst* has just lost her foretopgallant studdingsail, either from the force of the wind or from enemy fire—there are already holes in her topsails.

Here the battle is almost over. Both ships have lost their mizenmasts and the Frenchman's mainyard is gone in the slings; but they are still battering one another as fast as they can fire.

coast of Brittany, Captain Seymour (see page 48) caught sight of the *Thétis* slipping out of Lorient with an east-north-east wind, bound for Martinique. He at once wore in chase, and by cracking on sail he came up with her by about 9 p.m., although she was a flyer. The *Thétis*, running a good nine knots, suddenly shortened sail and luffed up, turning to rake the *Amethyst* with all her broadside guns. The *Amethyst* was having none of that: she swerved violently to port and then, the moment the French broadside was fired, to starboard, shooting up into the wind just abreast of the *Thétis*. And now began a furious cannonade, both ships battering one another at close range as fast as they could load and fire. The *Thétis*, as well as her extra guns, had 100 soldiers aboard, and they joined in with their musketry: the din was prodigious. After half an hour, when the *Amethyst* was a little ahead, the *Thétis* tried to cross under her stern and rake her, but there was not room and she ran her bowsprit into the *Amethyst*'s rigging amidships: in a few moments they fell apart, and still running before the wind they continued to hammer one another like furies. After another half hour of this the *Amethyst* forged ahead, put her helm hard astarboard, crossed the *Thétis*' hawse and raked her, the whole broadside sweeping the Frenchman's deck from stem to stern. Again they ran side by side, lighting up the night with their incessant fire; but at 10.20 the *Amethyst*'s mizenmast came down, smashing the wheel and sprawling over her quarterdeck. The *Thétis* shot ahead, meaning to cross and rake the *Amethyst* in her turn. But before she could do so, her own mizen went by the board. Once more the frigates were side by side, each hammering the other with a murderous fire. At 11 the *Thétis* had had enough: she steered straight for the *Amethyst* to board her. Captain Seymour saw that they would collide bow to bow and that the rebound would bring their quarters together. He gave the order not to fire. The ships struck, sprang apart, and then just before the Frenchman's quarter swung against the *Amethyst* he cried "Fire!" and the whole broadside tore into the *Thétis'* boarders as they stood ready to spring from her quarterdeck. She could only reply with 4 guns, and a moment later the ships were locked together, the *Amethyst*'s best bower anchor hooked into the *Thétis'* deck. So they lay for another hour and more, their guns still blazing furiously. The *Thétis* was set alight in many places, her fire gradually slackened, and at twenty minutes after midnight Captain Seymour called "Boarders away!", leapt aboard with his men and carried her at the point of the sword. A little later the Frenchman's two remaining masts fell over the side. Her hull was terribly shattered, and in her very courageous resistance she had lost 135 killed, including her captain, and 102 wounded. The *Amethyst* lost 19 killed and 51 wounded.

The comparative strength of the two frigates:

	Amethyst	*Thétis*
Broadside guns	21	22
broadside weight of metal	467 lb	524 lb
crew	261	436 (counting the 106 soldiers)
size	1046 tons	1090 tons

The rewards of victory were very great. The successful sea-officer enjoyed an honour, glory and popularity that no other man could earn. And after the great fleet actions the admirals were given peerages, huge presents of money and pensions of thousands a year; the victorious frigate-captain was made a baronet; first lieutenants were promoted commander and some midshipmen were given their commissions; but apart from public praise the rewards did not usually go much lower than that. For tangible advantages the ship's company looked to something else—to prize-money.

Whenever a man-of-war captured an enemy ship and brought her home she was first condemned as lawful prize and then sold. The proceedings were shared thus:

	before 1808	after 1808
Captain	$\frac{3}{8}$	$\frac{2}{8}$
Lieutenants, master, captain of Marines, equal shares of	$\frac{1}{8}$	$\frac{1}{8}$
Marine lieutenants, surgeon, purser, boatswain, gunner, carpenter, master's mates, chaplain, equal shares of	$\frac{1}{8}$	$\frac{1}{8}$
Midshipmen, lower warrant officers, gunner's, boatswain's and carpenter's mates, Marine sergeants, equal shares of	$\frac{1}{8}$ }	$\frac{4}{8}$ (in equal shares)
Everybody else, equal shares of	$\frac{2}{8}$	

Before 1808 the captain had to give one of his eighths to the flag-officers under whose orders he served: after 1808, one third of what he received. If he were not under an admiral he kept it all in both cases.

From the point of view of mere lucre, leaving honour and glory aside, it was not very profitable to take an enemy man-of-war: she was usually shockingly battered by the time she surrendered, and in any case she carried nothing but a cargo of cannon-balls and guns. To be sure, there was head-money of five pounds for every member of her crew, but real wealth, real splendid wealth, came only from the merchant or the treasure ship, laden with silk and spice, or, even more to the point, with gold and silver. An East-Indiaman was worth a fortune, and a ship from the Guinea coast, laden with gold-dust and elephants' teeth, meant dignified ease for life.

Back in 1743, when Anson, having rounded the Horn, having survived incredible hardships, and having sailed right across the Pacific, took the great Manilla galleon, he found 1,313,842 pieces of eight aboard her, to say nothing of the unminted silver. He brought it home, and 32 wagons were needed to carry it to the Tower of London: even a boatswain's mate had well over a thousand guineas for his share, while Anson, an admiral and a peer of the realm, was a very wealthy man.

And in 1762, when it became clear that a war with Spain was inevitable, cruisers were sent out: two of them, the *Active*, 28, and the *Favourite*, 20, had information of a register ship from Lima to Cadiz. As Beatson, the contemporary historian, says, they "had the good fortune to get sight of her on the 21st of May, and immediately gave chase. In a few hours they were close along-side, when Captain Sawyer hailed them whence they came; and, on being answered from Lima, he desired them to strike, for that hostilities were commenced between Great Britain and Spain. This was a piece of news they were not prepared for; but after a little hesitation, they submitted. Possession was then taken of the vessel, the *Hermione*, which was by far the richest prize made during the war; the cargo and ship, etc., amounting to £544,648 1s. 6d."

This splendid cake was cut up thus:

To the admiral and commodore	£64,963 3	9
Active's share		
captain	65,053 13	9
each commissioned officer	13,003 14	1
each warrant officer	4,336 3	2
each petty officer (this included midshipmen)	1,806 10	3
each seaman, etc.	485 5	4½

The *Favourite*'s share was £825 less, because she was not entitled to head-money for the 165 prisoners.

In 1804 much the same thing happened again: the Spaniards sent their treasure across the ocean, and off Cadiz there were four frigates of the Royal Navy waiting for it. It must be admitted that England had not formally declared

Unlike some admirals, Nelson never made a great fortune out of prize-money, but few equalled him in honours and none in glory. He was made a Knight of the Bath after St Vincent, a baron after the Nile and a viscount after Copenhagen. He was also Duke of Bronte in Sicily. He had many foreign decorations; and the Sultan of Turkey gave him the Order of the Crescent, together with a sable pelisse (particularly useful to a sailor) and the diamond-studded chelengk that he is wearing in his hat instead of the ordinary cockade. By the time of Trafalgar he had a fourth star; and as he had them all embroidered on his coat he was, alas, a conspicuous figure for a sharpshooter.

war, but they took it just the same. This time there was a fight, the Spanish ships being frigates of their navy, and in the course of it one most unfortunately blew up. The other three struck, and they were found to be carrying 5,810,000 pieces of eight. However, the Admiralty in an odd fit of conscience, decided that this was not lawful prize (although the frigates had been ordered to go and take it) and that the money, apart from a small proportion, should go to the Crown; so in the end the poor captains had to content themselves with a mere £15,000 apiece. Still, seeing that the captain of a sixth rate then earned just over £100 a year, they had made 150 years' pay in a morning, just as the seamen of the *Active* had made 36 years' in an afternoon; and in any case, there might always be another *Hermione* round the next headland.

There never was another *Hermione;* but splendid prizes were still to be made, and the very real possibility of a fortune lying just over the horizon, to be won by a bold stroke, a few hours' fierce action, added a certain charm to the sailor's hard and dangerous life at sea.

Songs

The beautiful working-songs and shanties of the merchant ships had no place in the Royal Navy, which was a silent service. But even so, there was music aboard a man-of-war: when the grog was served out the ship's fifer or fiddler played "Nancy Dawson", or "Sally in our Alley"; when the men were drummed to quarters it was to the tune of "Heart of Oak"; and when the anchor was being weighed the fiddler sat on the capstan and struck up "Drops of Brandy". And then of course there were the songs and ballads the sailors sang, particularly on a Saturday night at sea. Here is one of the most popular of them:

Farewell and adieu to you fine Spanish ladies,
Farewell and adieu all you ladies of Spain,
For we've received orders to sail for old England
And perhaps we shall never more see you again.
　　We'll rant and we'll roar like true British sailors,
　　We'll range and we'll roam over all the salt seas,
　　Until we strike soundings in the Channel of old England—
　　From Ushant to Scilly 'tis thirty-five leagues.

We hove our ship to when the wind was sou'west, boys,
We hove our ship to for to strike soundings clear,
Then we filled our main-tops'l and bore right away, boys,
And right up the Channel our course we did steer.

    We'll rant and we'll roar, etc.

The first land we made is known as the Dodman,
Next Ram Head near Plymouth, Start, Portland and Wight;
We sailèd past Beachy, past Fairley and Dungeness,
And then bore away for the South Foreland light.

    We'll rant and we'll roar, etc.

Then the signal is made for the Grand Fleet to anchor
All all in the Downs that night for to meet,
So stand by your stoppers, see clear your shank-painters,
Haul all your clew-garnets, stick out tacks and sheets.

    We'll rant and we'll roar, etc.

Now let every man toss off a full bumper,
Now let every man toss off a full bowl,
For we will be jolly and drown melancholy
In a health to each jovial and true-hearted soul.

    We'll rant and we'll roar, etc.

And here is part of a home-made ballad, one of the many composed and sung by sailors:

I'll tell you of a fight, boys, and how it did begin.
It was in Gibraltar Gut, which is nigh unto Apes' Hill;
It was three privateers that belonged unto Spain
Who thought our British courage for to stain.

I'll tell you, brother sailors: it was on a calm day,
Then one of the privateers they boarded us straightaway:

They hove in their powder-flasks and their stink-pots,
But we repaid them with our small shot.

They being in number three hundred and more,
And is not equal, you'll say, unto threescore:
But now I will tell you the courage of our men,
That we valued them not, if they had been ten.

Our small arms did rattle, and our great guns did roar,
Till one of them we sank, and the other run ashore;
Such a slaughter we made as you seldom shall see,
Till an hundred and eighty we drown'd in the sea.

Our fight being over, and our fray being done,
And every man then scowering his gun,
And every man to a full flowing bowl;
Here's a health to all British loyal souls.

My name is George Cook, the author of this,
And he may be hang'd that will take it amiss.

And here is another, about the action between HMS *Nymphe* and the French frigate *Cléopâtre* in June 1793:

Come, all you British heroes, listen to what I say;
  'Tis of a noble battle that was fought the other day;
  And such a sharp engagement we hardly ever knew:
  Our officers were valiant and our sailors so true.
  The *La Nymphe* was our frigate, and she carried a valiant crew,
  With thirty-six twelve-pounders, that made the French to rue.
  At daylight in the morning the French hove in sight;
  Captain Pellew he commanded us in this fight.

Full forty eighteen-pounders we had for to engage;
  The French they thought to confound us, they seemed so much
    enrag'd.
  Our captain cry'd, "Be steady, boys, and well supply each gun;

HMS *Téméraire*, a 98-gun second-rate, earned her reputation at Trafalgar, where she sailed into action immediately astern of the *Victory*. In the murderous, confused battle that followed she supported the Admiral, engaging several ships, often two or three at a time, boarded and captured the *Fougueux*, and then took the gallantly-fought *Redoubtable*, whose musketry had just killed Nelson; but the *Téméraire* paid heavily for her triumph, losing no less than 47 men killed and 76 wounded—close on one in five of her crew. A generation after Trafalgar, when steam was beginning to kill sail, she was scrapped. A tug, belching smoke, towed the Fighting *Téméraire* away to the breaker's yard; Turner painted this picture in 1839.

We'll take this haughty Frenchman, or force her for to run!"

The action then began, my boys, with shot on every side;
They thought her weight of metal would soon subdue our
  pride.
I think the second broadside her captain he was slain,
And many a valiant Frenchman upon the decks were lain.

We fought her with such fury, made every shot to tell,
And thirteen brave seamen in our ship there fell,
Tho' forty-five minutes was the time this fight did last,
The French ship lost her tiller and likewise her mizen mast.

Then yard arm and yard arm we by each other lay,
And sure such noble courage to each other did display;
We form'd a resolution to give the French a check,
And instantly we boarded her off the quarter-deck.

Her colours being struck, my boys, she then became our prize,
And our young ship's company subdued our enemies,
Altho' they were superior in metal and in men.
Of such engagements you may seldom hear again.

And now in Portsmouth Harbour our prize is safely moor'd.
Success to all brave sailors that enter now on board;
A health to Captain Pellew, and all his sailors bold,
Who value more their honour than misers do their gold.

Which is not a bad note on which to finish a short account of
the Royal Navy of Nelson, St Vincent, Duncan, Howe,
Cochrane, Seymour and a hundred thousand other true-
hearted seamen.

Index

References to illustrations are in italic figures